Greeks Built Temples

and Other Questions About Ancient Greece

Fiona Macdonald

Kingfisher

NEW YORK

KINGFISHER
Larousse Kingfisher Chambers Inc.
95 Madison Avenue
New York, New York 10016

First edition 1997
10 9 8 7 6 5 4 3 2 1
Copyright © Larousse plc 1997

LIBRARY OF CONGRESS CATALOGING-IN-PUBLICATION DATA
Macdonald, Fiona.
   I wonder why Greeks built temples and other questions about
ancient Greece—Fiona Macdonald
       p.   cm.—(I wonder why)
   Includes index.
   Summary: Questions and answers introduce the clothing, food,
weapons, religion, and other aspects of daily life in ancient Greece.
   1. Greece—civilization—To 146 B.C.—Juvenile literature.
[1. Greece—civilization—To 146 B.C.—Miscellanea. 2. Questions
and answers.]
I. Title. II. Series. I wonder why (New York, N. Y.)
DF215.M145 1997
938—dc20 96-34095 CIP AC

ISBN 0-7534-5056-9
Printed in Italy

Series designer: David West Children's Books
Author: Fiona Macdonald
Consultant: Louise Schofield
Cover Illustration: Chris Forsey
Cartoons: Tony Kenyon (B.L. Kearley)

CONTENTS

4 Who were the ancient Greeks?

5 Why did Greece grow bigger and bigger?

6 Was Greece one big happy country?

7 Where did the citizens take charge?

7 Where did the clock go "drip-drip?"

8 Who were the fiercest soldiers?

9 Who paid for weapons and armor?

10 Why did ships have long noses?

11 Why was it easier to travel by sea?

12 Who was goddess of wisdom?

13 Who told stories about the gods?

14 Who listened to the trees?

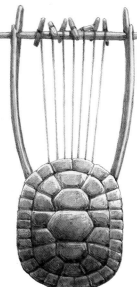

15 Where did Greeks empty their wine?

16 Why did Greeks build temples?

17 Whose fingers made their fortune?

18 When did a couple get married?

19 What did girls do all day?

19 Who went to the gym every day?

20 Why were Greek clothes so comfy?

21 Why were Greek sandals bouncy?

21 Who took a shower in a bowl?

22 Where could you buy sweet-smelling cheese?

23 Why did the Greeks beat their trees?

23 What did the Greeks have for breakfast?

24 Why did actors wear masks?

25 How did a turtle make music?

26 Why were the Olympics held?

27 Did the winners get medals?

27 Who ran the first marathon?

28 Why did doctors ask so many questions?

28 Who had his best ideas in the tub?

29 Who discovered that the Earth is round?

30 How do we know about ancient Greece?

31 Who copied the Greeks?

32 Index

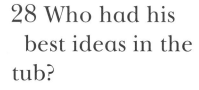

Who were the ancient Greeks?

The ancient Greeks were people who lived from around 3,000 B.C. to 140 B.C. They didn't live only in Greece—some of them lived to the north and the east, in lands that we now call Bulgaria and Turkey. Others lived on small rocky islands in the Aegean Sea.

● Many Greeks set sail for North Africa, Turkey, Italy, and France. They found safe harbors where they built new towns, and they cleared the land for farming.

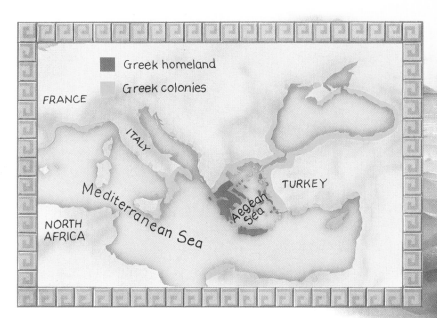

Greek homeland
Greek colonies
FRANCE
ITALY
Mediterranean Sea
NORTH AFRICA
Aegean Sea
TURKEY

● By 500 B.C. the Greek world was large, rich, and powerful. It stretched from France in the west to Turkey in the east.

● Wherever they went, the Greek settlers took their own way of life. They must have looked strange to the locals!

● The Greeks were smart people. They had good laws and strong armies. They built beautiful temples and theaters. They were great thinkers, artists, and athletes.

Why did Greece grow bigger and bigger?

Greece started off as a small country, and much of its land was too rocky for farming. By about 750 B.C., there was little room left for new towns or farms, and food began to run short. Because of this, many people left Greece to look for new places to live, and the Greek world began to grow.

Was Greece one big happy country?

Ancient Greece was not a single country as Greece is today. It was made up of different states—cut off from each other by mountains, valleys, or the sea. These states weren't much bigger than cities, but each had its own laws and army, and often quarreled with its neighbors. Athens was the largest city-state.

• Each state was made up of a city and the surrounding countryside. Many city-states lay close to the sea and had a harbor, too.

HARBOR

TEMPLE

PRISON

AGORA

SCHOOL

CITY WALLS

FARMLAND

Where did the citizens take charge?

- Sparta was a city-state in southern Greece. It was ruled by two kings from two royal families, helped by a council of wise old men.

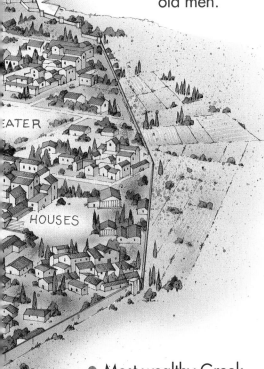

In Athens, only grown men who weren't slaves were citizens. They could choose their government officials and vote for or against new laws. Citizens could also speak at the Assembly. This was a huge open-air meeting where people stood up and told the government what it should be doing.

- There had to be at least 6,000 citizens at every Assembly. They met on the slopes of a hill in Athens and voted by raising their hands.

- Most wealthy Greek households had slaves. The slaves did all the hard work, such as building, farming, housework, and taking care of children.

Where did the clock go "drip-drip?"

Citizens who spoke at the Assembly weren't allowed to drone on for too long. Each speaker was timed with a water clock. When the last drop of water had dripped from the jar, his time was up. He had to sit down and hold his tongue!

Who were the fiercest soldiers?

The soldiers of Sparta formed the fiercest army in ancient Greece. They were brave, ruthless, and very well trained. None of the men had ordinary jobs, even in peacetime. Their whole lives were devoted to training and fighting.

● Spartan warriors were known for their long, flowing hair. Before a battle, the soldiers carefully combed their "manes." Perhaps this made them feel as brave as lions!

● Bravery was very important to Spartans. They punished cowardly soldiers by shaving off half their hair and half their beard—a terrible disgrace.

Who paid for weapons and armor?

- Greek soldiers fought side by side in tight rows. This formation was called a phalanx. Each soldier's shield overlapped his neighbor's, making a strong, protecting wall.

Greek soldiers had to buy their own weapons and armor. A wealthy soldier bought himself a sharp spear and sword, a strong shield, and expensive body armor. But a poor soldier made do with whatever he could find—sometimes this was little more than an animal skin and a wooden club!

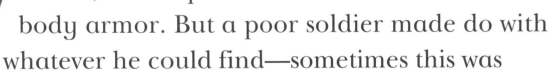

- In Sparta it wasn't just the men who had to be fit. Women did lots of exercises to make sure their babies were born healthy and strong.

- After winning a battle, soldiers sometimes offered gifts of their armor in thanks to the gods. They laid the armor inside a temple or hung it on the branches of a tree.

Why did ships have long noses?

Greek warships had a long battering ram at the front, below the prow. In battle it could be deadly. The oarsmen rowed as fast as they could toward an enemy ship and tried to smash a hole in its side with the ram. With any luck, the enemy ship would sink and its crew would drown.

● Most Greek ships had a big eye painted on either side of the prow. The sailors hoped that these piercing eyes would scare away evil spirits and protect the men until they were safely home.

- The biggest warships, called triremes, had three rows of oarsmen along each side of the boat. With 170 men pulling on the oars, ships zipped through the water at an amazing speed.

- Each ship had a flute player who piped a tune and thumped a beat with his feet. The oarsmen rowed in time to this rhythm, so they didn't get all tangled up!

Why was it easier to travel by sea?

Because mainland Greece was mountainous and wild, people often traveled from one part to another by sailing around the coast. This was much quicker and easier than struggling up steep, stony tracks on the back of a weary donkey.

Who was goddess of wisdom?

Athena was the goddess of war and also of wisdom—her symbol was the wise owl. She had special powers to protect the city of Athens, too, and the citizens loved and worshiped her. They built Athena a temple, called the Parthenon, high on the Acropolis—a hill overlooking the city.

● According to legend, the gods lived on top of Mount Olympus, the highest mountain in Greece. But they didn't always behave as you'd expect gods to —they spent a lot of their time quarreling!

Hermes, messenger of the gods

Zeus, king of the gods

Demeter, goddess of crops

Aphrodite, goddess of love and beauty

Hera, queen of the gods, goddess of women and children

Hades, god of the underworld

- The Greeks believed in many different gods and goddesses. Each one had different powers. Some of the gods were kind, but others were stern and cruel.

Who told stories about the gods?

A famous poet named Homer told exciting stories about gods and heroes. His poem *The Odyssey* tells of Odysseus, a Greek soldier sailing home to Ithaca from the war with Troy. The sea god Poseidon tries to sink his ship, but with Athena's protection, Odysseus finally gets home.

- **Poseidon**, god of the sea, tried to sink Odysseus's ship by stirring up violent storms.

- Inside the Parthenon stood a towering statue of Athena—about ten times taller than you! It was covered with gold and ivory.

Who listened to the trees?

The Greeks believed that nature goddesses, called dryads, lived deep in the woods. Priests and priestesses guarded these holy places and prayed to the dryads. Then they would listen hard for rustlings in the trees, which they believed were messages in reply.

● According to legend, dryads wore crowns of leaves and danced in the woods. They also carried axes—to attack anyone who damaged their trees.

● There were over 40 religious holidays in Athens each year. There are paintings of these festivals on wine jars and other Greek pottery. People loved festivals. They had time off work and plenty of free food and drink.

● Wealthy people took animals to the temple to be sacrificed to the gods. Poor people couldn't afford to take live animals—so they took pastry ones instead.

Where did Greeks empty their wine?

Many Greeks prayed to the gods in their own homes at a special altar. They liked to offer the gods gifts of food or wine. Sometimes, worshipers poured a whole jar of wine over the altar. More often, they drank most of the wine themselves and left only a tiny drop for the gods!

Why did Greeks build temples?

The Greeks built temples as homes for their gods. They made these buildings as magnificent as possible, using the finest materials and the very best craftsmen, to please the gods. Elegant statues, tall columns, and painted friezes decorated the outsides. Inside, the rooms were filled with treasures.

● The Parthenon in Athens was built out of dazzling white marble. The huge stone blocks were carried to the building site on ox-drawn carts and hauled into position with ropes and pulleys.

Whose fingers made their fortune?

Greek craftsmen were very skilled, and made beautiful works of art. Stonemasons carved marble figures. Metalworkers made statues and vases out of bronze. Potters made wonderful jars and flasks. These craftsmen often became rich and famous, overseas as well as at home.

● Greek potters were famous for their beautiful bowls, vases, and cups. They worked with artists who decorated the pots with red or black paintings of gods, heroes, or ordinary people.

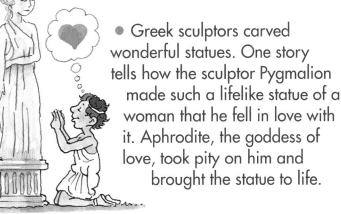

● Greek sculptors carved wonderful statues. One story tells how the sculptor Pygmalion made such a lifelike statue of a woman that he fell in love with it. Aphrodite, the goddess of love, took pity on him and brought the statue to life.

● Temple columns weren't made from a single piece of stone. They were built out of drum-shaped pieces held together by pegs. The pieces fit together snugly—as long as they were put in the right order!

When did a couple get married?

Usually when their parents told them to! A wealthy father wanted a good match for his son or daughter—to make his family even richer and more important. Greek brides were often just 13 or 14 years old. Their grooms were usually much older— about 30, at least.

● On her wedding day, the bride was driven to her new husband's home in a chariot. There was laughter and music, and burning torches to light the way.

● After the wedding, the bride's chariot was broken. This meant she could never go back to her old home.

What did girls do all day?

Young girls didn't go to school, though a girl from a rich family might have a home tutor. Most girls just learned how to spin fleece into thread, and then weave it into fine woolen cloth. Greek women made all the cloth for their families' clothing, wall hangings, blankets, and rugs.

● One Greek legend tells the story of a girl named Arachne, who believed she was better at spinning than the goddess Athena herself. Athena was so angry that she turned Arachne into a spider. Then all she could spin was a web!

● A few women did learn to read and write. One of the most famous Greek poets was a woman named Sappho, who lived about 2,500 years ago.

Who went to the gym every day?

"Gym" is short for "gymnasium," the Greek name for school. Boys went to school from the age of about seven. They learned all the usual things like reading, writing, and arithmetic, and how to give a speech, recite poetry, and sing.

Why were Greek clothes so comfy?

The Greeks wore light, loose-fitting clothes. There were no buttons or zippers, just flowing robes or simple tunics called *chitons* (pronounced KY-tuhns). Chitons were big squares of cloth, held in place by pins at the shoulders and a belt around the waist.

● The Greeks liked brightly colored clothes decorated with embroidery. Most clothes were made out of wool or linen, but wealthy people wore silk, too.

● Greek women liked to wear a lot of jewelry. Wealthy women wore gold and silver bracelets, necklaces, and long dangly earrings that jingled with every move.

Why were Greek sandals bouncy?

Most Greeks liked to go barefoot in the house. But outside they wore warm boots in winter and cool sandals in summer. The most comfortable sandals had thick cork soles, which made them soft and bouncy—perfect for walking on stony ground.

● To protect themselves from the hot summer sun, the Greeks wore broad-brimmed hats made of woven straw.

Who took a shower in a bowl?

When Greek people took a shower, they undressed and crouched inside a deep pottery bowl. A slave would then come and pour jars of cool, refreshing water over them.

Where could you buy sweet-smelling cheese?

Town-dwellers bought their food at the *agora*, the open-air market in the center of town. There was always plenty of fresh fruit, vegetables, and grain—all grown on farms just outside town. They could also buy cheese made from goat's or sheep's milk, which was flavored with sweet-smelling herbs.

● Farmers loaded their donkeys with food to sell at the *agora*—fruit and vegetables, cheese, chickens, and a squealing piglet or two!

● Every year after the grape harvest, people had to jump into big wooden tubs and crush the fruit into juice to make wine. It was hot, tiring, and sticky work.

Why did the Greeks beat their trees?

Before farmers harvested their olives, they spread huge sheets of cloth under the trees. Then they beat the branches to make all the ripe fruit fall onto the cloth. This was much quicker and easier than trying to pick the tiny olives one by one!

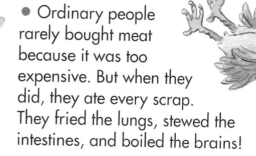

● Ordinary people rarely bought meat because it was too expensive. But when they did, they ate every scrap. They fried the lungs, stewed the intestines, and boiled the brains!

What did the Greeks have for breakfast?

Favorite Greek breakfast foods included bread, cooked barley, eggs, fish, or figs. Some Greeks even drank wine for breakfast—but mixed with plenty of water. Others preferred to drink milk.

Why did actors wear masks?

Only boys and men were actors. They wore masks so that the audience could see what part they were playing—a man or a woman, a wise person or a fool. Greek theaters were huge, with seats for up to 17,000 people. Spectators at the back couldn't always see the actors' faces. But the big, colorful masks were easy to see.

● Some plays lasted all day. The audience took cushions and blankets to put over the hard stone seats, and brought food and wine in case they felt hungry or thirsty.

● Greek theaters stood on sloping hillsides. Their semicircular shape helped carry the actors' voices right to the back—even when they whispered!

How did a turtle make music?

Sadly, only a dead turtle could make music. An empty turtle shell was used to make a lyre—a musical instrument similar to a harp. Musicians attached strings to the shell and plucked them to play a tune.

● The double flute was a popular musical instrument, but it was difficult to play. You needed twice as much breath as for a single flute, and each hand played a different tune.

● Theater staff carried big sticks in case of trouble. Sometimes the huge audience got excited by a play and began to riot. A few hefty whacks soon quieted them down!

Why were the Olympics held?

The Olympic Games were part of a religious festival in honor of Zeus, king of the gods. Every four years, 20,000 people flocked to Olympia to watch athletes run, box, wrestle, and drive chariots in races. The hardest event was the *pentathlon*. Contestants took part in five events—the long jump, running, wrestling, and throwing the discus and javelin.

● Women were banned from the Olympics, but they took part in games of their own in honor of Hera, queen of the gods.

● The Olympic athletes were always naked! The Greeks were proud of their bodies, and liked to show them off.

Did the winners get medals?

To win at the Olympics was a great honor, just as it is today. But there were no medals given in the ancient games. Instead, the winners got crowns made of laurel leaves, jars of olive oil, beautiful pots or vases, and wool, silk, or linen to make into clothes.

● Greek boxers didn't wear padded gloves like boxers today. They simply wrapped strips of leather around their fists.

Who ran the first marathon?

In 490 B.C., the Greeks won a battle at Marathon, about 26 miles from Athens. A Greek soldier named Pheidippides ran all the way to Athens to tell the citizens the good news. Sadly, his "marathon" exhausted him, and the poor man collapsed and died.

● There was no marathon race in the ancient games, but there is today. It measures roughly 26 miles—the same distance that Pheidippides ran 2,500 years ago.

Why did doctors ask so many questions?

Greek doctors knew it was important to find out as much as they could about their patients. They asked them all kinds of questions—what foods they ate, whether they exercised, and so on. People had once believed that illness was a punishment from the gods. Greek doctors had more scientific ideas.

● Greek doctors were clean, well dressed, and cheerful. This made their patients trust them and the doctors knew this helped people to get better more quickly.

Who had his best ideas in the tub?

Archimedes was a mathematician who lived in Greece around 250 B.C. One day, while taking a bath, he finally figured out a problem that had been troubling him for ages. He was so excited that he jumped out of the tub shouting "*Eureka*!" ("I've got it!") and ran to tell his friends!

• The Greeks loved to learn about new ideas. They would sit under a shady tree and talk for hours about all kinds of things—from the way people lived to the future of the world.

Who discovered that the Earth is round?

Greek scientists were very interested in the Earth and space. In about 470 B.C., a scientist named Parmenides was watching an eclipse of the Moon. He noticed that the Earth cast a curved shadow on the Moon, and figured out that if the shadow was curved, then the Earth must be round.

• Diogenes was a famous Greek thinker. He lived in an old wooden barrel so people could see that he didn't care about money or being comfortable. He was only interested in ideas.

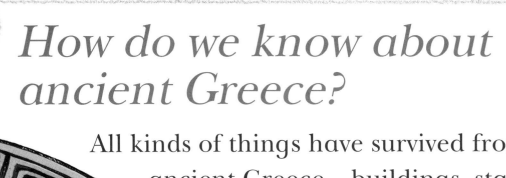

How do we know about ancient Greece?

All kinds of things have survived from ancient Greece—buildings, statues, writings, weapons, jewelry, pottery, and coins. Historians study these things carefully. They look for clues to piece together a picture of the past—just as detectives look for clues in a case.

● Greek pottery tells us a lot about life in ancient Greece. It is decorated with pictures of families at home, athletes, festivals, and people at work. Can you guess what job the man on this plate did?

- Ancient Greece began to lose its power around 300 B.C. In 148 B.C., armies of the Roman Empire invaded Greece and soon took control.

Who copied the Greeks?

About 2,000 years ago, the Romans invaded Greece. They conquered its armies and added its lands to their own empire. But Roman people respected the Greek way of life. They admired Greek poetry, plays, buildings, and art. They copied many Greek ideas and used them to improve their own way of life.

- The Acropolis is a high rocky hill in the center of Athens. At the top is the heart of ancient Greece. Beautiful buildings stand all around you, including the Parthenon—the temple built for the goddess Athena between 447 B.C. and 432 B.C.

- Greek temples have survived for nearly 2,500 years. But today they're being damaged by air pollution, which eats away the stone.

Index

A
Acropolis 12, 31
actors 24
agora 6, 22
Aphrodite 13, 17
Arachne 19
Archimedes 28
army 5, 6, 8–9, 31
Assembly 7
Athena 12–13, 19, 31
Athens 6–7, 12, 15, 16, 27, 31
athlete 5, 26, 30

B
building 4–5, 7, 16, 30–31

C
chariot 18, 26
chiton 20
citizen 7
city-state 6–7
clothing 19, 20–21, 27
craftsmen 17

D
Demeter 13
Diogenes 29
doctors 28
dryads 14

E
entertainment 15, 24–25

F
farming 4–5, 6–7, 22–23
flute 11, 25
food 5, 15, 22–23, 24, 28
festivals 15, 30

G
gods 9, 12–13, 14–15, 16–17, 26, 28

H
Hades 13
harbor 4, 6
Hera 13, 26
Hermes 13
Homer 13

J
jewelry 20, 30

L
lyre 25

M
Marathon 27
marriage 18
mask 24
Mount Olympus 12

O
Odysseus 13
olives 23
Olympics 26–27

P
Parmenides 29
Parthenon 12–13, 16, 31
phalanx 9
Pheidippides 27
poetry 13, 19, 31
Poseidon 13
pottery 15, 17, 27, 30
Pygmalion 17

R
ram 10
Romans 31

S
sandals 21
Sappho 19
school 6, 19
science 28
ship 10–11
slaves 7, 21
soldier *see* army
Sparta 7, 8–9
sports 26–27
stonemasons 17
statue 13, 16, 17, 30

T
temple 5, 6, 9, 12, 15, 16–17, 31
theater 5, 7, 24–25
transportation 10–11
trireme 10–11

W
warship 10–11
water clock 7
weapons 9, 30
weaving 19
wine 15, 22–23, 24

Z
Zeus 13, 26